Tolerance and Ha
in Britain

Understanding and combating prejudice

Written by Christopher Yeates

Illustrated by Zoe Sadler

Note to teachers:

The content of this book expands and elaborates on the themes presented in the Key Stage 2 series by the same author. In some places the text and accompanying illustrations from the Key Stage 2 books are reproduced here verbatim, or in very similar form.

© Gresham Books 2017
Published by Gresham Books Limited
The Carriage House, Ningwood Manor, Ningwood,
Isle of Wight PO30 4NJ
ISBN 978-0-946095-89-6

Printed in Great Britain

CONTENTS

BRITISH VALUES

Britain is made up of England, Wales and Scotland, and the people who live in these countries are called British. The people of Northern Ireland may also call themselves British and together we make up the United Kingdom. This book is to help you learn about and come to understand some of the British Values we all share.

INTRODUCTION

Critical thinking – how to read this book

In this book you will be asked to debate and evaluate situations and then decide what you think. When you debate, evaluate and decide, you are using your powers of critical thinking.

Learning to become a strong critical thinker will help you think clearly and rationally about what to believe, say, write and do.

The processes of critical thinking provide you with a series of steps to help you analyse, evaluate, debate and decide what you think about situations or choices for yourself.

Step 1: Analyse

What are the facts of the situation or choice?
How do you know the facts are true? Is there any evidence? Is the evidence trustworthy?

Step 2: Debate

Consider all points of view – especially if you disagree – and let everyone have their say. Do you have reasons to support your views? Is there evidence to support your point of view or that of others? Do you think this evidence is strong or weak?

Step 3: Keep an open mind

Are you being open-minded? Are you prepared to listen to the reasons of others and change your mind if their reasons are persuasive? Being prepared to be open-minded is an essential part of becoming a strong critical thinker.

Be honest with yourself. Check for prejudice. Are you being prejudiced? Are others being prejudiced?

Step 4: Evaluate

What are the strengths and weaknesses of the arguments behind each point of view? How strong is the evidence supporting these arguments?

Step 5: Decide

Reflecting on every point of view, and the reasons and evidence you have heard, decide what you think.

To double-check whether you have genuinely been open-minded, ask yourself:

- What is the strongest reason supporting your decision?

- What single piece of evidence helped you decide?

- What reason or piece of evidence might change your mind?

What we mean when we say...

Evaluate: identify the strengths and weaknesses.
Analyse: examine something in detail.
Evidence: facts provided to help prove something is true or false.
Prejudice: a preconceived opinion that is not based on facts or personal experience.

CHAPTER 1: IMAGINE ALL THE PEOPLE

Let's face it: you're unique. Have a really good look at the person sitting next to you. See what colour their eyes are, and how far they are apart. See what colour their skin is, and whether they have any freckles. Are both their ears the same size? Try and notice as much as you can.

It's pretty amazing to think that nobody else in the whole world has exactly the same face as the person you were looking at. Also, that nobody else in the whole world has the same face as you do. And that's just for starters. Nobody else in the world has exactly the same thoughts as you. Nobody else in the world has exactly the same family and friends as you do. Nobody else in the world knows exactly what it's like to be you. Everybody in the world is a little bit different to everyone else, and this makes each of us unique.

For a rather small island, Britain has a lot of people with different backgrounds, talents, beliefs and cultures. Our country has every sort of person you can imagine. Old people. Young people. Big people. Small people. Dark-skinned people. Light-skinned people. People who are good at sport. People who can cook. People who can play music. People who can draw. Funny people. Serious people. Clever people. Kind people. People who pray every day, and people who don't. We could go on and on.

Nobody is more important or less important than anybody else. In fact, everybody is *equally* important. We call this idea *equality*. Equality makes sure that everybody is treated *fairly*, and has the same *opportunity* to make the most of their lives and special talents. Ideas about equality are going to crop up quite a bit in this book, so keep an eye out for them. And always remember: everyone is **different**. Everyone is **unique**. And everyone is **important**.

What we mean when we say...

Equality: making sure that everyone is treated fairly, and given the same opportunities to make the most of their lives and talents.

Fair: treating people in the same way.

Debate and evaluate:

In a group, discuss:

1 Why does equality matter?

2 Can you think of any situations where you feel an individual, or a group of people, has been treated unfairly?

3 How do you think people can be persuaded to treat others fairly?

Read, research and decide:

1 Carry out your own research and write a page about a group of people who have not been treated fairly or equally in the past by our country. Find out why this group was not treated equally. Is this group being treated fairly today? For example, you could research the struggle that women had to be allowed to vote.

2 Explain why it would be unfair to decide whether someone can do a job or not based only on their age. Do you think that people over the age of 60 face prejudice from employers? Try to provide examples or evidence to support your views.

CHAPTER 2: WHAT'S IN A CULTURE?

In Britain we have lots of different *cultures* existing side by side. A culture unites the ideas and traditions of a group of people who share a similar background, and do similar things together. Everybody is part of a culture. In fact, many people are part of more than one culture.

Have a think about your own cultural background. You might feel it includes the **languages** you speak at home and at school. You might feel it includes the way you **dress**, the way you express yourself by the clothes you wear. You might feel it includes the **music** you enjoy listening to, the television programmes you watch, or the **sports** you enjoy watching and playing. You might feel it includes the sort of **food** you eat, or if you're lucky, have prepared for you at home. Other parts of your cultural background might be your **religious faith**, or a sense of **tradition**. *Tradition* is the word we give to our knowledge of stories, skills and ways of life that have been passed down to us from our *ancestors* (our families).

All of these different things go into making up your cultural background. Having lots of different cultures existing side-by-side makes our country an incredibly exciting, interesting place to live. 'Multi' means 'lots of'. Britain has lots of different cultures, so it makes sense to say that Britain is *multicultural*.

What we mean when we say...

Culture: the ideas, traditions and activities of a group of people.

Tradition: the passing on of stories, skills and ways of life from generation to generation.

Debate and evaluate:

In a group, discuss:

1 Discuss the many different cultures that you might be a part of. These might include your own family's culture, or that of groups that you belong to through friends or other interests, for example, a sports team, as well as cultures that stem from your beliefs, religious faith or national culture.

2 What are the benefits of belonging to more than one culture?

Read, research and decide:

1 Write about some of your family's traditions. For example, do you always celebrate Christmas or go to see a fireworks display on Bonfire Night? Or watch the X Factor on a Saturday night? What benefits do you think come from celebrating these traditions?

2 Write about one of your school's traditions. Do you think this tradition is beneficial to your school community? Remember to support your views with examples or evidence.

CHAPTER 3: FROM ANCIENT GRUDGE TO MULTICULTURAL BRITAIN

Some people think that it is only recently that Britain has had lots of different people and cultures. This is not correct, however, as our country has been **multicultural for a very long time** – over 2000 years, in fact. Even very early in our island's history, the many **Iron-Age tribes** were made up of different cultures and ways of life. These tribes are sometimes called the Celts, but they came from all across Europe and did not share a common identity.

When the **Romans** invaded, around 2000 years ago, our country was changed forever, and for the next 1000 years, invasions by **Anglo-Saxons**, **Vikings** and, in 1066, the **Normans**, continued to mix many different cultures from all over Europe together.

Each of these groups had different languages, buildings, laws, faiths, and traditions. Amazingly, the ways of life and ideas of these ancient people still play a very active part in many of our own cultures today.

What we mean when we say...

United Kingdom (UK): England, Wales, Scotland and Northern Ireland.

Britain: the island of Britain made up of England, Wales and Scotland.

Iron-Age Tribes: the many different tribes who lived in Britain during the Iron Age.

Romans: a powerful people who controlled a huge empire. They ruled England for about 400 years.

Anglo-Saxons: tribes from Germany, Holland and Denmark who lived in Britain from around 410 to 1066 AD.

Vikings: fierce raiders and traders from Scandinavia.

Normans: in 1066 they invaded England, led by William the Conqueror, who thought he should be King of England.

Debate and evaluate:

In a group, discuss:

1 The Romans invaded our country around 2000 years ago, and the Normans invaded England in 1066. How do you think a culture changes when a new group brings its own beliefs and ways of living? Make a list of the problems and opportunities that an invading culture might bring to an existing community.

Read, research and decide:

1 Carry out your own research and identify some ways that either the Romans or the Normans are still influencing the way we live in Britain today. For example, the Normans brought their castle-building skills to England. Can you think of any examples to do with our language or architecture?

2 From your research do you think that our country has benefitted from either the Roman or the Norman invasion? Use examples and evidence to support your ideas.

CHAPTER 4: TODAY'S MULTICULTURAL BRITAIN

Some people have arrived in Britain as *refugees*. A refugee is somebody who has been forced to escape their own country, because it is **not safe** for them to live there. Some have had to escape famine, such as people from Ireland during the *Irish Potato Famine* around 150 years ago. Others have had to escape war. For example, during the *Second World War* (1939–1945), many Jewish refugees fled countries such as France, Poland, Austria and Germany, because their lives would have been in danger from the Nazis if they had stayed. More recently, refugees have come to Britain, fleeing from war and danger in countries such as Syria, Iraq, Afghanistan, Pakistan, Rwanda, and many others around the world.

Many more people have arrived in Britain as *migrants*. A migrant is somebody who moves to another country to **live and work** there. Since the Second World War, many migrants have come to Britain from *Commonwealth* countries. The Commonwealth is made up of 52 countries that used to be part of the *British Empire* before they gained independence. During the Second World War, millions of men from Commonwealth countries fought side by side with Britain. After the War, many were invited and encouraged to come and work in this country to help rebuild Britain after the damage caused by six years of war. Migrants came from different parts of Asia, Africa, the West Indies, and lots of other places all over the world.

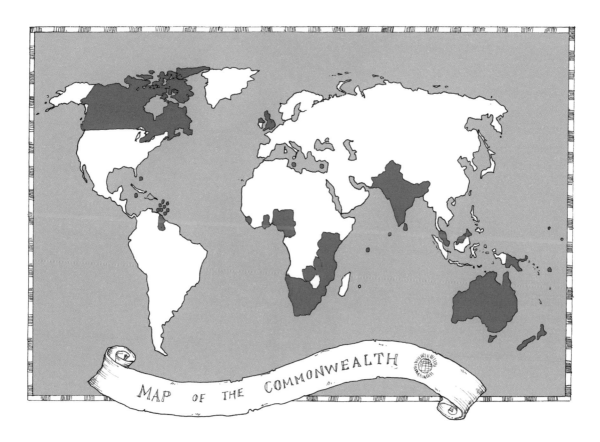

MAP OF THE COMMONWEALTH

Migrants to Britain brought their special cultural backgrounds to share with the multicultural society that already existed here. Many of these new arrivals had children, who also had children, who had children themselves, and so on. In fact, it is possible you are one of those who might be able to trace your roots back to somewhere else in the world. But no matter whether your family has roots in another country, or your family has lived in Britain for a long time, always remember: everyone is different. Everyone is unique. And everyone is important.

People from closer to home have also joined our multicultural society since the Second World War. There are people living and working in Britain from every single country in Europe. To give you an idea of how multicultural our country is, there are at least 300 different languages spoken in London every day. 300!

You can think of our multicultural society as being like an **orchestra**, or a band with lots of different musical instruments. Each culture is like a different instrument; it looks different, it sounds different, and it has to be played and looked after in its own special way. But here's the thing: all the instruments in the orchestra are **playing the same piece of music together**. And the piece of music? Well, it's our country, our world!

When people come to Britain to live, it is called *immigration*. But the traffic is not all one way. When people leave Britain it is called *emigration*. For example, while Britain was busy encouraging people from the Commonwealth to move here after the Second World War, Australia was doing the same thing at the same time – but to British people! They promised houses and jobs to British people who emigrated to Australia to start a new life. There are British people living and working in nearly every single country you can think of across the world.

What we mean when we say...

Refugee: somebody who has been forced to escape their own country because it is not safe.

Migrant: somebody who moves to another country to live and work.

The Commonwealth: a group of 52 countries across the world which used to be part of the British Empire before they gained independence.

Debate and evaluate:

In a group, discuss:

1   Do members of your group have family members or relations living in other countries, or ancestors from another country? What challenges do you think someone faces if they move to a new country?

2   Why do you think that people move to other countries to live or work?

Read, research and decide:

1   Write a paragraph explaining in your own words the difference between a refugee and a migrant. Carry out your own research and provide an example of both a refugee and a migrant coming to Britain.

2   All countries have a duty to accept refugees. Write a page explaining whether you agree with this statement. Remember to provide examples or evidence to support your point of view.

CHAPTER 5: HOW DOES DISCRIMINATION BEGIN?

Everyone is unique, and everyone is important. And if everyone is important, it makes sense that everyone should be treated fairly and as equals. Sadly, not everyone sees it this way. Instead, some people choose to **discriminate**.

Discrimination is treating a person, or groups of people, unfairly. Discrimination is often seen against people of different races or religions, or sometimes against people because of their age or gender, or perhaps because of some kind of disability. In the UK discrimination is against the law.

Discrimination can range from making somebody feel unwelcome and excluding them from activities and opportunities, to verbally and physically abusing them or things they stand for. Discrimination thrives on poisoning the differences between people, rather than celebrating them. As we have seen, each and every one of us is different; no two people are the same. This means that **discrimination can happen to anybody**. Throughout history, people have been discriminated against because of the colour of their skin, their accent, how their body looks or works, their religion or beliefs, what gender they are, or how old they are.

Some of this discrimination has been because it suited some people to behave as if their abilities, beliefs, culture, or even country, was better than others. A good example of this is the *transatlantic slave trade*, where millions of Africans were enslaved by Western countries. Another example is discrimination against women, where until around 100 years ago women were not allowed to vote in the UK, and many other countries, because men believed that women were intellectually inferior.

It's a tricky idea, but one worth trying to understand. Everyone is different, and we should celebrate and enjoy this diversity. But difference should not be a reason to think of somebody who looks a bit different, or speaks a bit differently, or thinks a bit differently, as 'alien' to you. If you had two apples, and one was a red apple and one was a green apple, would you say one of them was not an apple, or 'more' of an apple than the other one? Of course not. They are both apples. We don't talk about a red or green 'race' of apples, and neither should we talk about different 'races' of human beings. **There is only one race: the human race**.

Discrimination has led to some of the most horrific crimes in human history, such as *genocide*. But of course, discrimination starts with the little things – unkind jokes in the classroom, casual comments in the street – and these little, nasty things can add up to big, appalling things. This is why discrimination is against the law in the UK and why each and every one of us has a responsibility to understand discrimination, and lead by example in helping to stamp it out.

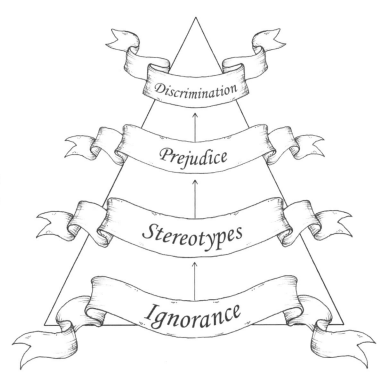

But how does discrimination begin? Discrimination starts with ignorance about the beliefs, culture or circumstances of others.

1: As we can see, discrimination begins with **ignorance**. Ignorance means that you don't know about something, or don't understand it. People can sometimes be scared of things they do not understand, and be suspicious of them. People can also *think* they know about something, but be wrong about it – perhaps because they have been taught to think a certain way, or have become **prejudiced** by other people's opinions.

2: Being ignorant about something that seems different can lead to people making **assumptions**. An assumption is something that we believe without having evidence or proof. It is then far too easy for an assumption to become a **sweeping generalisation**. A sweeping generalisation is when we decide that something must be the same in every case and do not allow for any exceptions. Quite often people make sweeping generalisations about people from a certain country. Making this kind of generalisation leads to **stereotyping**. There are damaging and unfair stereotypes for just about everything – from physical appearance to religious beliefs. For example, you have probably heard rivals from another school generalise and stereotype pupils from your school. This is likely to be very misleading as everyone in your school is different with their own strengths and weaknesses.

3: Stereotyping leads to people being **judged**. Where discrimination is concerned stereotyping works in a negative way by creating **prejudice**. Prejudices **label** people, and ignore what that person is really like and what makes them unique. Prejudice leads to damaging and dangerous feelings of 'us' and 'them'. For example, in the 1930s and during World War Two the Nazis made some terrible and untrue generalisations about the Jews in Germany. Making these generalisations, and creating prejudice against the Jews, made it easier for the Nazis to send millions of Jews to concentration camps.

Prejudices usually don't make sense. Do you think it makes sense to think, 'I once saw a person with blue eyes steal a car, so I'm going to stay away from my classmate with blue eyes'? Presumably not – and yet that is the sort of mistake people make every day, based on surface features such as skin colour, gender, or religious belief. The fact that people share a culture, do similar things together and share special days together does not make them the same. It is not correct to pre-judge all Christians, Muslims, Buddhists, or Welsh people as all being the same, just as it is not correct to pre-judge all people who have a pet goldfish as being the same!

4: Discrimination does not happen by accident. As we can see, discrimination is the result of **ignorance leading to stereotyped and prejudiced opinions**. Discrimination is an action, a type of behaviour.

In the UK, it is **illegal** for somebody to be treated differently or be harassed because they have a different nationality, religion, or skin colour, or because of their age or sex.

What we mean when we say...

Discrimination: the unjust or unfair treatment of a person or culture, especially on the grounds of their race, age or gender.

Ignorance: lack of knowledge or information about something.

Prejudice: a preconceived opinion that is not based on facts or personal experience.

Sweeping Generalisation: making a general judgement about something based on insufficient evidence.

Stereotype: a widely held but fixed and oversimplified image or idea of a particular type of person or thing.

Debate and evaluate:

In a group, discuss:

1 Are there any groups of people that you think people hold stereotyped views about? For example, some people 'stereotype' politicians as being dishonest. Why do you think such stereotypes are unfair?

2 Prejudice means holding an opinion about something that is not based on facts, evidence or personal experience. Can you think of anything that you might be prejudiced about? What might help you stop being prejudiced?

3 What can you do to help stop discrimination?

Read, research and decide:

1 Look carefully at the diagram on page 15 and write a paragraph explaining in your own words how ignorance can lead to discrimination.

2 Carry out your own research on a country, or group of people, that you previously knew very little about. In what ways has your research changed the views or ideas you previously held?

3 Write a paragraph explaining how knowing more about a country, or group of people, helps prevent discrimination. Use your research to provide examples to support your ideas.

CHAPTER 6: FOUR STEPS TO HELP CHALLENGE DISCRIMINATION

Step 1 – Educate yourself

If discrimination begins with ignorance, the obvious place to begin tackling it is with education. A big part of this will come from school, and learning about the world around you and how it works. Hopefully, however, your school will teach you something even more important: **how to think for yourself**. A lot of people's prejudiced ways of thinking are passed on to them from the **media**, from the **Internet**, from **films**, sometimes even from their families and friends. It is very easy simply to accept these ideas, and never understand that everyone is different and important.

Thinking for yourself involves **challenging** assumptions and stereotypical ways of thinking. It involves **questioning** the stories you are being told and the **labels** you are being shown. Whenever you are being told about a person, or a culture, ask yourself:
* How much evidence am I being given to support this view?
* Am I being told the whole story?
* Is what I am being told fair, and not based on assumptions or prejudice?

Step 2 – Talk about it

Talking about things is one of the best ways of understanding them. Discussions which are **open-minded** and **inclusive** help people to appreciate what makes cultures unique, and encourages **respect** for other people's points of view.

It is likely that during a discussion about different cultures, you will not agree with everything that is being said. That's okay! Not everyone has to agree on an issue, just like not everyone has to support the same football team. In fact, it would be a bit dull if they did! The important thing is that you **listen** to all points of view, and **respect** another person's right to hold a point of view, just as they should listen to, and respect, your own point of view.

Step 3 – Ask questions

There is also nothing wrong with not knowing something, or not understanding it, which is why it is always okay to ask **questions**. It is far better to ask somebody something about their culture, than to remain ignorant and make assumptions. They will probably enjoy explaining it to you! Talking about things in this way will also help people see for themselves how much different cultures have in **common**.

Step 4 – Take responsibility and challenge discrimination

Taking responsibility for dealing with discrimination involves understanding that every **action**, and every **word**, no matter how insignificant it might seem, has **consequences**. It also involves understanding that it is not enough simply not to discriminate against people yourself. **Standing up** and **speaking out** against discrimination wherever you see it – in the classroom, out of school, on the sports field – is vital if we want to make our society a happy, peaceful, exciting place to live.

Taking responsibility also involves understanding that we are always part of a bigger community of people. No person, and no culture, exists in **isolation**, and we all have a responsibility to look after the communities we are a part of. You are part of a family community, a school community, a town community, a national community, and a global community of countless remarkable people and cultures and traditions.

Taking responsibility means that if you really want things to change, and really want to tackle discrimination and inequality, you can lead by example and **be the change you want to see**. If you do this, others will follow you. **It starts with you**.

Debate and evaluate:

An excellent way of challenging discrimination is to be inspired by the example of role models. Role models can come in lots of different shapes and sizes. It could be a parent, a teacher, a singer, a sports star, a politician – anyone who has broken down barriers between people and helps to make the world a fairer, more respectful, more joyous place to live.

In a group, discuss:

1   Make a list of role models that inspire you. Can you explain why?

2   Agree three ways in which you could challenge discrimination.

Read, research and decide:

1   Some of the most famous role models are those who spent their lives fighting for equal rights for people who were being discriminated against. Research one of the following and explain how their actions have helped combat discrimination:
   • Nelson Mandela
   • Anne Frank
   • Martin Luther King Jr.
   • Rosa Parks
   • Emmeline Pankhurst

2   Write a paragraph explaining how you can challenge discrimination.

CHAPTER 7: RELIGION AND TRADITION

Religion can be an important factor in a person's cultural background. In the UK, the biggest religion is **Christianity**, with a number of different *denominations* (or branches) such as *Anglicanism* (the official religion of England) and *Catholicism* making up the church as a whole. The next biggest religion is **Islam**, followed by **Hinduism**, **Sikhism**, **Judaism** and **Buddhism**. Being an active member of a religious community is likely to play a big part in your daily routine, in the way you treat others, and the way you think about the world around you.

Even if you are not religious, however, it might surprise you to learn just how much of your cultural background would be very different without the *traditions* that come from marking special days in religious calendars. For example, whether or not you follow the teachings of Jesus, you have a Jewish preacher who lived 2000 years ago in Israel to thank for your two week holiday at Christmas time. It is also easy to forget that whether we follow a religious code or not, what many of us think of as 'right' and 'wrong' can be traced back to the teachings of scripture and holy books from all over the world.

Christianity

42 million people in Britain today describe themselves as Christian, and around six million actively practise the Christian faith.

Christianity is centred on the life and teachings of Jesus Christ who was born in the Middle East over 2000 years ago. Christians believe Jesus Christ is the Son of God. Christians' holy book is the Bible which is divided into two sections: the Old and New Testaments. Christians worship in churches.

The most important Christian festivals are Lent, Easter and Christmas. Whether you are Christian or not you will probably have taken part in a number of Christian festivals or traditions.

You may have had an 'Advent calendar' counting down the days to Christmas Day. You have probably sent Christmas cards to your friends, or received Christmas presents. Christmas Day celebrates the birth of Jesus in Bethlehem, over 2000 years ago.

You may well have eaten pancakes on Pancake Day. Pancake Day is on Shrove Tuesday, traditionally the day when Christians used up foods that they would not be eating during Lent. Lent is the 40 days before Easter when Christians believe that Jesus went into the desert to fast and pray. Lots of people give things up for Lent – like chocolate.

Easter is the most important celebration in the Christian calendar. For Christians, Easter celebrates the day when Jesus rose from the dead, three days after he died on the cross.

Islam

Followers of **Islam** are called Muslims. There are over two and a half million Muslims in Britain. Muslims believe that the universe was created by God, who they call Allah, and that human beings have been placed on Earth to worship Allah, and to obey his will. Muslims also believe that around 1400 years ago in **Mecca** (Makkah), Saudi Arabia, Allah's will was revealed to Muhammad. Muhammad is Islam's most important **prophet**. For Muslims, Allah's teaching is contained in their holy book, the **Qur'an**, which was written by Muhammad after the Angel Gabriel *revealed* to him the word and will of Allah. The Qur'an is written in **Arabic**, an ancient language still spoken by millions of people across the world today. A mosque is the Muslim place of worship, for which the Arabic word is *masjid*.

Ramadan is a special month for Muslims because they believe it is the month in which the Prophet Muhammed began to have the Qur'an revealed to him. Fasting during the month of Ramadan is called *sawm*. The end of Ramadan is marked by a joyous celebration called Eid al-Fitr – the Festival of the Breaking of the Fast.

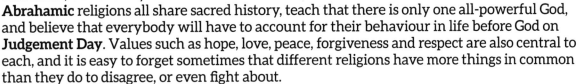

Like all religious traditions, fasting during Ramadan has a spiritual and personal meaning. Fasting is intended to help teach Muslims self-discipline and generosity. It reminds them that all things in life come from Allah, and should not be taken for granted. It also helps them to understand the suffering of the poor, who never have enough to eat. Fasting does not apply to people who are sick, to small children, or to pregnant women, and it is also acceptable to fast, but to take essential medicine at the same time.

Muhammad is Islam's most important prophet, but not its only one. Like Christians and Jews, Muslims also follow the teachings of prophets such as **Abraham, Moses**, and **Jesus** – though they do not believe that Jesus is the Son of God. Prophets are not the only thing that Islam, Christianity and Judaism have in common. These three **Abrahamic** religions all share sacred history, teach that there is only one all-powerful God, and believe that everybody will have to account for their behaviour in life before God on **Judgement Day**. Values such as hope, love, peace, forgiveness and respect are also central to each, and it is easy to forget sometimes that different religions have more things in common than they do to disagree, or even fight about.

Diwali: A Special Time for Hindus and Sikhs

Every year, Diwali is one of the biggest festivals in the world, central to several different religions including **Hinduism** and **Sikhism**. The word 'Diwali' means 'rows of lighted lamps', and is also called the **Festival of Lights**. Diwali usually falls in October or November, and lasts for five days, with the fourth day marking the Hindu New Year.

Diwali celebrates the **triumph of good over evil**, and light over darkness. To symbolise this, Hindus and Sikhs light up their houses and streets with **candles** (*diyas*), light up the sky with **fireworks**, and decorate their houses with beautiful **rangoli**. A rangoli is an intricate, very colourful floor pattern made with powder or coloured rice.

Diwali for Hindus

For Hindus, Diwali is a time to honour **Lakshmi**, the Hindu Goddess of wealth and prosperity. Lakshmi has four arms, and brings happiness and good luck wherever she goes. For this reason, Hindus are keen for Lakshmi to visit them, and so welcome her into their homes with candles, rangoli, and doors and windows left open for her entry. Hindus also offer prayers in their place of worship (called a **mandir**), and make offerings (called **puja**).

Diwali is also a time for Hindus to celebrate the **legend of Rama and Sita**. The story goes that Prince Rama and his wife, Sita, were banished from their home in Ayodhya by the King and sent to live in the forest for 14 years. After several years of happiness, Sita was kidnapped by the evil demon **Ravana**, who sported 10 heads and 20 arms. But Ravana's numerical advantage was no match for the magic arrows of the warrior Rama and his army of monkeys. Rama slew Ravana, rescued Sita, and they both returned triumphant to Ayodhya, guided by rows of **lighted lamps**, to be crowned King and Queen.

Diwali for Sikhs

Diwali is important to Sikhs because it commemorates **Guru Hargobind's** release from prison in 1619. Guru Hargobind is one of the **Ten Sikh Gurus**, whose writings teach Sikhs how to live and what to believe.

Passover: A Special Time for Jews

Jewish people trace their ancestry back to the three ancient *Patriarchs*: **Abraham**, his son **Isaac**, and his grandson **Jacob**. The **covenant** (or agreement) made between Abraham and God around 3800 years ago marks the beginning of Jewish history. The covenant says that in exchange for God's protection and love, Jews must keep God's laws and bring holiness into every part of their daily lives.

One of the most important ways in which God acted on behalf of his chosen people was to lead them out of slavery in Egypt, in the time of the Pharaohs.

Passover is one of the most important festivals in the Jewish year. The Passover Festival helps Jewish people remember how the Children of Israel left slavery when Moses led them out of Egypt over 3000 years ago.

In the UK, Passover celebrations last for eight days. To prepare for Passover, Jewish homes are cleaned thoroughly from top to bottom, and all traces of leaven bread (*chametz*) are symbolically removed. Jewish life revolves around the family and the wider Jewish community, so Jews try to spend as much time as possible during the Passover period with family and close friends. For the first two nights of Passover, this takes the form of special ritual feasts called **Seders**. Several generations are usually present, as well as guests, who sometimes are strangers in need of kindness.

What we mean when we say...

Prophet: a special messenger who is sent by God to teach people how to live good and obedient lives.

Qur'an: the Islamic holy book believed to be the word of God as told to the Prophet Muhammad by the Angel Gabriel.

The Abrahamic Religions: an Abrahamic religion is a religion which follows the belief that the Hebrew patriarch Abraham and his descendants hold an important role in human spiritual development. The best known Abrahamic religions are Judaism, Christianity and Islam.

Mosque: a Muslim place of worship.

Rangoli: an intricate, very colourful floor pattern made with powder or coloured rice.

Mandir: a Hindu place of worship.

Synagogue: a Jewish place of worship and instruction.

Debate and evaluate:

In a group, discuss:

1   What impact do you think religious festivals and traditions have had on your life?

2   In a number of religions followers are expected to fast – give up certain foods – for a period of time. What benefits do you think come from giving something up for a time?

3   Have you ever joined in with a religious celebration from another religion? What did you learn from this experience?

Read, research and decide:

1   Write a paragraph about a religious tradition or festival that has had an impact on your life. What did this experience teach you?

2   Research a festival or tradition from another religious faith. How do followers of this religion celebrate this event? What does it teach them? Try to find someone from this religion that you can interview to tell you more about their experiences.

CHAPTER 8: TRADITIONS AND PATRON SAINTS

England, Scotland, Wales and Ireland each have special patron saint days. On these days, the patron saint is remembered and different parts of the national culture are celebrated.

Saint George – Patron Saint of England

St George's Day, celebrated on 23 April, is a special day to celebrate St George and the values he represents of English ideals of honour, valour and gallantry.

On St George's Day, it is customary to wear a **red rose**, the emblem of England. St George's personal emblem is a **red cross** which is also the English national flag. People fly the English flag to show their support for England.

George is commonly shown on horseback, slaying a **dragon**, a legend used to inspire English knights during the Hundred Years War against France in the Middle Ages. Born in Turkey, St George was himself a soldier in the Roman Army, and died as a martyr under torture after refusing to deny his Christian faith.

St George is remembered in church services on the Sunday closest to 23 April. These nearly always include the hymn '**Jerusalem**', written by the poet William Blake. Other customs include parades, which may feature **morris dancing** (an English folk dance), and **Mummers' Plays**, an ancient English pantomime tradition which tells the story of St George and the dragon.

Saint David – Patron Saint of Wales

On 1 March, people in Wales celebrate Welsh culture and the life of their patron saint, **St David**. St David lived around 1400 years ago as a Celtic monk, who travelled widely across Wales to preach Christianity and established several monasteries.

To celebrate St David's Day, people might attend a special church service, colourful parade, or traditional **eisteddfod** – a festival of Welsh poetry and music. They eat a lot of **cawl** (leek soup), and take care to pin a **daffodil** or **leek** to their clothes, as these are both Welsh emblems. It was St David himself who issued the famous advice to Welsh soldiers fighting the Saxons to stick a leek in their cap so they could tell friend from foe – clearly a handy tactic, as the Welsh won the battle!

Saint Andrew – Patron Saint of Scotland

St Andrew's Day is celebrated on 30 November, and is a day for celebrating the best of Scottish food, music and dress.

St Andrew was one of Jesus Christ's twelve **disciples**. The bones of St Andrew are believed to have been brought to Fife, on the Scottish coast, where today the town of St Andrew's stands.

Like Jesus, and also St George, St Andrew died a martyr, crucified by the Romans on a diagonal cross called a **saltire**.

Today, the St Andrew's Saltire is Scotland's national emblem, and appears on Scotland's national flag which is flown on St Andrew's Day. St Andrew's Day celebrations might include a **ceilidh** dance, probably to the accompaniment of **bagpipes**. St Andrew's Day is also a good time for a taste of Scotland's national food: **haggis**, a meat dish perhaps washed down with a **whisky** – the Scottish are world-famous for their whisky.

Ceilidhs, bagpipes, haggis and whisky are also regular features of **Burns Night**, an annual festival marked around the world to celebrate the Scottish poet Robert ('Rabbie') Burns. His most famous work is **Auld Lang Syne**, which is sung in many countries on New Year's Eve.

Saint Patrick's Day – Patron Saint of Ireland

On 17 March, the people of Ireland and the Irish around the world wear their greenest finery and celebrate St Patrick's Day. St Patrick's Day is celebrated with parades, dancing and special foods.

St Patrick brought Christianity to Ireland. He was born in Roman Britain, but was kidnapped by Irish pirates when he was 16 and taken to work in Ireland as a slave for six years. He escaped back to his family, but later returned to Ireland as a priest and missionary.

It is said that St Patrick used a **shamrock**, a three-leaved plant, to explain the Christian Trinity of the Father, the Son, and the Holy Spirit. Today, the shamrock is the national flower of Northern Ireland, and the green plant is worn on St Patrick's Day.

St Patrick's Day is celebrated in more countries around the world than any other national festival. Americans even have the tradition of pouring enough vegetable-based dye into the Chicago River to turn it completely green.

25

What we mean when we say...

Eisteddfod: a festival of Welsh poetry and music.

Shamrock: a small three-leaved green plant used as the national emblem of Ireland.

Martyr: a person who dies for their beliefs.

Saltire: a diagonal cross in the shape of an X, used as the national emblem of Scotland.

Ceilidh: a party with Scottish or Irish folk music and singing, traditional dancing, and storytelling.

Haggis: a traditional Scottish meat dish made from sheep's heart, liver and lungs mixed with onion, oatmeal, suet and spices and wrapped in a sheep's stomach.

Debate and evaluate:

In a group, discuss:

1 Events such as the Olympics, or Rugby or Football World Cups, remind us all of our national identity. Why do you think we enjoy supporting our own national team?

2 The United Kingdom comprises the countries of England, Scotland, Wales and Northern Ireland. Citizens of the United Kingdom are all British, but we might also identify closely with our own country within the United Kingdom. Do you think of yourself as English, Scottish, Irish, Welsh or British, or from another country altogether? Explain why.

Read, research and decide:

1 Write a paragraph explaining when you feel most British. For example, this might be when you are supporting a national team, or taking part in some kind of national celebration. Give examples to support your ideas.

2 Do you feel as if you are part of more than one national culture, for example, British and Welsh, or British and English, or British and another country altogether? Write a page explaining when you feel part of these cultures.

CHAPTER 9: OTHER SPECIAL DAYS AND CELEBRATIONS

Some celebrations started as a result of an event or belief, and provide good fun for family and friends. Here are some you might recognise.

Halloween – 31 October

Halloween is celebrated every year on 31 October. Some think it began with the ancient **Celtic** festival **Samhain**. As autumn gave way to winter at Harvest time, the **pagan** Celts believed that an opening to the world of the dead meant that for one night a year, evil spirits could roam at will in our world. This is where the idea of dressing up as a grisly ghost comes from; the wily Celts reasoned that if you look like a ghost, the real ghosts will think you are one of their own and leave you alone!

Others think that Halloween has always been part of marking **Christian festivals for the dead**. Whatever its origins, the word Halloween comes from hallowed (or holy) evening. The day after Halloween is **All Saints' Day**, where Christians remember the numerous saints no longer with us. The day after that is **All Souls' Day**, when Christians remember all those who have died.

Regardless of exactly where Halloween came from, Halloween has become a night of dressing up as ghosts, witches or other scary figures especially for children. Part of the traditions of Halloween include putting a pumpkin in your window, hollowed out and carved to show a grinning face when a candle is put inside. The candle is intended to scare away any evil spirits!

Guy Fawkes or Bonfire Night – 5 November

'Remember, remember, the fifth of November,
Gunpowder, treason and plot!'

If you've ever heard this rhyme before, you will probably already know that Bonfire Night commemorates the discovery of a plot to blow up King James I as he opened Parliament on 5 November, 1605. Those plotting to kill the King hid barrels of gunpowder in a cellar under the Houses of Parliament, but a secret letter warned the King and his Government about the plot. Though not the leader of the plot, **Guy Fawkes** was found guarding the gunpowder. After three days of torture in the *Tower of London*, Fawkes named his fellow gang members and was then sentenced to death.

King James encouraged people to light **bonfires** to celebrate the failure of the plot, a tradition which survives today along with the burning of a 'guy' on top of the fire and **big firework displays**.

New Year's Eve

New Year's Eve is celebrated on 31 December all over the world. In Britain, like elsewhere, people gather to see the old year out and to welcome the new year in. As the clock strikes midnight there are often fireworks and celebrations to mark the first moments of the new year.

Chinese New Year

The date for Chinese New Year changes each year, but always falls between 21 January and 20 February. Each new year is named after one of 12 animals in the **Chinese zodiac cycle**.

Chinese New Year is celebrated in cities throughout the UK with special food, and a **lion dance**. Chinese New Year is also marked by a good deal of **red clothing**, **red lanterns**, **gold lettering**, and of course, **fireworks**. Some believe that the noise of fireworks and the colour red scare away demons and evil spirits.

What we mean when we say...

Samhain: an ancient pagan Celtic festival which marked the end of the harvest season and the beginning of winter.

All Saints' Day: a Christian festival celebrated on 1 November to remember all saints.

All Souls' Day: a Christian festival celebrated on 2 November to remember all those who have died, especially one's relatives.

Chinese Zodiac: a system based on a 12 year cycle, with each year named after an animal.

Debate and evaluate:

In a group, discuss:

1 Have you been to a Guy Fawkes fireworks display or a New Year's Eve party? Why do you think people enjoy celebrating these occasions together?

Read, research and decide:

1 Britain is a multicultural society. Research a festival that has been brought to Britain by another national culture and explain how it is celebrated. For example, you could write about Chinese New Year.

CHAPTER 10: SHARING VALUES

Sharing and commemorating special days helps us to share our beliefs and values, and make our values clear to one another. Such days also remind us of the great sacrifices and hardships suffered by individuals in service of our country.

Harvest Festival

Harvest Festival celebrations take place towards the end of September and are celebrated in schools and churches all over Britain. They give thanks for the harvest that has been successfully grown and collected, and also celebrate all of the hard work that this has involved.

It is thought that the tradition of giving thanks for the harvest in church began on 1 October 1843, when Rev. Robert Hawker held the first Harvest Thanksgiving Service in his Anglican church at Morwenstow in Cornwall. He wanted people to say 'thank-you' to God for the harvest; his actions created a tradition that we still recognise today.

Today, we take for granted that we have enough to eat in Britain. Many years ago a poor harvest meant that there would not be enough food for a community and many would go hungry, or even starve to death.

Celebrating a successful harvest helps us to appreciate what we have and to remember those who are not as fortunate as we are. Harvest Festival also helps us to understand that many good things need a lot of hard work and determination.

Remembrance Day – 11 November

Remembrance Day, also known as Armistice Day, is a very special day for people throughout our country. On 11 November, many Britons wear a poppy to show that they are remembering the dead who have died for our country. Poppies were chosen because these red flowers grew up on the battlefields of the First World War.

Armistice Day marks the end of the First World War in 1918, at 11am on the 11th day of the 11th month. Every year, a two-minute silence is held at 11am to remember the people who have died in wars. Remembrance Sunday, which usually falls on the second Sunday in November, also gives us the chance to remember those who have died in wars, as well as the terrible loss and harm that war brings.

Debate and evaluate:

In a group, discuss:

1   Consider the harvest celebrations that you celebrate at school. What kind of values do you share?

2   Why do you think that Remembrance Day is such an important day in our national culture?

Read, research and decide:

1   Carry out your own research on what Remembrance Day means to people of different ages. Interview friends, your teacher or members of your family and ask them what Remembrance Day means to them.

DO YOU REMEMBER?

Let's finish by reminding ourselves of some of the most important points we've learned:

- It is very important to be a critical thinker; this means being prepared to keep an open mind, take time to analyse and check the facts of a situation, consider more than one point of view and only then decide what you think.

- Everyone is unique and everyone is important. Everybody is part of a culture and many people are part of more than one culture. Your culture is made up of everything to do with how you live.

- Our country has been multicultural for over 2000 years. Lots of people and cultures mixing together in Britain is nothing new.

- Everyone who has settled in the UK has brought their special cultural backgrounds.

- Some people have arrived in Britain as refugees and some as migrants.

- Discrimination is treating a person, or groups of people, unfairly.

- Discrimination is the result of ignorance which can lead to stereotyped and prejudiced opinions.

- To prevent discrimination it is important to educate yourself, discuss issues and ask questions.

- It is very important to take responsibility and challenge discrimination when you hear or see it.

- Religion can be an important part of a person's cultural background. Christianity is the biggest religion in Britain. Islam is the second biggest religion in Britain.

- Lots of people take part in Christian festivals and religious events even if they are not Christian, for example, celebrating Christmas, eating pancakes on Shrove Tuesday or giving up something for Lent.

- Different religious festivals and traditions play a very important part in the lives of millions of people.

- Special days celebrating the patron saints St George, St David, St Andrew and St Patrick are also a time to celebrate the national cultures of England, Wales, Scotland and Ireland.

- Other special days like Armistice Day (Remembrance Day) help people share important values.